PENUMBRA
Poems about Dementia

Elizabeth Miller

Penumbra
Poems about Dementia
© 2019 Elizabeth Miller

emillerpoetry@gmail.com

All rights reserved. No part of this book may be reproduced in any form or by any electronic or mechanical means, including information storage and retrieval systems, without permission in writing from the publisher, except by reviewers, who may quote brief passages in a review.

Original artwork © 2019 Lara Geach

Foreword

Dementia brings a range and depth of emotion that can be bewildering, both for the person living with it, and for those close to them. The feelings dementia generates for friends and family members can be unfamiliar, challenging and complex. Identifying and articulating what you are going through can be difficult; yet being able to name an emotion is a step towards learning to cope with it.

Elizabeth's poems shed light on the experience of dementia, in ways that elucidate the emotional journey families face. By telling the story of her mother's dementia through beautifully articulated descriptions, Elizabeth helps us understand better how dementia changes life for the person living with it and those who support them. She takes us through the early days of recognising a person's failing cognitive abilities, right to the palliative end stages of dementia, as we accompany her on a poetic pilgrimage that lasts years.

There is much about the experience of dementia that remains a mystery. We cannot know what is happening in the mind of a person in the later stages. This makes poetry an ideal medium for expressing the lived reality, hinting at what might be happening and using metaphor to explain what is observed, while striving to maintain connection with the person.

If you, like Elizabeth, are trying to understand dementia as you journey alongside a person you care about, these poems will help you make sense of the emotions that may be present. Her reference to Bible passages will bring hope and comfort. If, like me, you want to grasp something of what life is like for the person with dementia and those close to them, Elizabeth's poetry will help you empathise.

Read the poems first and let them speak to you. Then read

Elizabeth's helpful notes which provide the context for each poem. This collection of poems makes a profound contribution to our quest to understand dementia better. It is both moving and compelling in giving a voice to the unspoken cries of the heart of those affected by dementia.

Julia Burton-Jones
Anna Chaplaincy Lead and Dementia Specialist
Diocese of Rochester

The Gift of Years

Rochester Diocese
Anna Chaplaincy

Acknowledgements

The creation of 'Penumbra' has been a team effort.

Firstly, I would like to express my gratitude to my parents, June and Alan, for encouraging me to appreciate literature and enjoy writing, even from an early age. My thanks go to my siblings, Ian, Jane and Patrick, for their practical and emotional support while sharing the journey through our mother's dementia. Thank you, too, to my sister, Cathy for reading me stories and helping to make my earliest years so much fun.

Other family members have encouraged me in writing 'Penumbra' - in particular my youngest daughter, Rosie, who helped with the proofreading. John, Emily and Bridget have also been supportive. Special thanks should go to Julia Burton-Jones for recognising the potential of my poetry to help others, for writing such a lovely foreword and for promoting the 'Penumbra' collection of poems within the diocese of Rochester. I would also like to thank my vicar, Canon Mandy Carr, for keeping me positive by giving so much encouragement and wise advice.

To all those who have read 'Penumbra' in its manuscript form and offered feedback - including Shirley Hayes and Sarah Griffiths - I express my gratitude. Linda Young has also proved to be an efficient proofreader, in addition to giving advice and helping me believe in myself. I would also like to thank Cathrin Beddoe for her guidance about marketing. Many more friends, including Jennifer Harper, Sharon Abbas and Moya Grady, together with others I meet at church and in our village community, have been positive about my efforts, giving me extra motivation to proceed with this book.

Special mention should go to Lara Geach, for creating such inspired and original artwork for a wonderful cover design.

And finally, I want to thank God for inspiring me, lifting my spirits and blessing all our efforts.

Why 'Penumbra'?

Having written most of this collection, I came across the word 'penumbra' and believed it would make a suitable title. Light and dark are frequent themes in these poems. Thinking that the partial shadow of a penumbra could apply to the difficulties caused by dementia, I was later surprised to learn that the word can be used as a medical term to refer to the area surrounding an ischemic event, such as a stroke. This confirmed to me that 'Penumbra' would be an appropriate title.

The word 'penumbra' can also mean an indeterminate group which could represent those who care for someone with dementia, particularly as they might be perceived by the person with the illness. Partial shadow suggests not total gloom but a sadness alleviated by some joy and peace.

Introduction

About six months after my mother had moved into a care home, I was struggling to come to terms with what was happening to her. Some of my anxiety resulted from the realisation that I could now do little to rebuild the broken relationship I had with my mother. Conversely, the effects of dementia were driving us further apart.

I decided to start putting my thoughts down on paper. It

was many years since I had written poetry and my skills were rusty. Soon, I discovered that this writing had a cathartic effect. However dark the subject matter, I was gaining a sense of satisfaction in creating some 'beauty from ashes' and this served to benefit my emotional and spiritual health.

At one time, I felt that writing poetry about dementia was almost becoming an obsession. The turning point came when I forced myself to write two more uplifting poems about my mother. At this stage, I felt that I could let the theme go for a while and soon I found myself writing poetry on a myriad of other subjects, which felt liberating.

Poetry has continued to pour out of me. I have told friends that it was as if God had turned on a power shower and left it running! At times, it has been clear to me that He is using me as a channel; I feel compelled to share this gifting and do so generously, in love. If I can help someone who has struggled as I have, if I can walk alongside someone to show them that they are not alone in their difficulties, then this will make all the effort worthwhile.

Elizabeth Miller
April 2019
Sevenoaks Weald

Contents

Foreword	3
Acknowledgements	5
Why 'Penumbra'?	7
Introduction	7
Poems and Notes	11
The Map	11
More Than One Problem	13
Knowing	16
Birthday	19
You Just Have To Laugh	21
Home Visits	24
Water Resistant	27
Leave Me Alone	29
Dream Time	31
Who Are You?	33
The Lights Are Too Bright	35
Thinking...Thinking	38
A Thief In The Night	41
Looking For Signs	43
Mother Asleep	45
Turn Off The Lights	47
In The Care Home	49
Letting Go	51

Low Tide	53
Thursday's Child	56
Your Hands	59
Waiting For The Inevitable	61
Remembering	63
Your Hand In Mine	66
Questions	68
Connection	71
Items Of Value	74

The Map

We were rambling along
Chatting and joking
Helping each other
Over stiles
Through thickets
And muddy patches.

The map?
We had a map before.
We thought it showed the way.
Did someone drop it
Where the land
Rose more steeply?
Did anybody see it fall?

Before us now
An angry knot of tangled paths
Beneath a darkening sky.
But which to take and
Who to lead the way?

The Map

When my three siblings and I first began to realise that our mother was struggling with her memory and thinking skills, we were quite cheerful and positive about her future. We began to adopt strategies to overcome obstacles and make life easier for her. These early days are referred to in the lines, 'Chatting and joking / Helping each other / Over stiles...' Here the mood is upbeat.

On many occasions during my mother's illness, we have seemed to be 'on the back foot'. No sooner have we formulated a plan of campaign, than a deterioration in her condition has made it invalid. It was as if we thought we had a map but then suddenly realised that we had mislaid it. This idea led to my choice of 'The Map' as the title and extended metaphor for this poem.

A crisis occurs, when the map is lost, 'Where the land / Rose more steeply'. The mood of the poem becomes more sombre and there is a suggestion of potential conflict in the words 'angry' and 'Beneath a darkening sky.' Using the metaphor, 'An angry knot of tangled paths', emphasises the complexity of the problem and the frustration which it creates. Questions serve to unsettle the reader further. They highlight the feelings of uncertainty and disorientation which carers and those with dementia often experience, as they try to come to terms with a changing landscape.

When I feel bewildered, I often ask God for His help in discerning the best way forward; this can be seen as an answer to the poem's final question. The following words from Proverbs have helped me to gain a better sense of perspective and direction.

"Trust in the Lord with all your heart
and lean not on your own understanding;
in all your ways submit to him,
and he will make your paths straight"

(Proverbs 3:5-6, New International Version)

More Than One Problem
So, what appears to be the problem?
The doctor's rodent eyes peered out
Above his rimless spectacles,
Flicked up to the clock
And back again.
Don't worry, I thought,
I have read the sign in the lobby –
'Book a double appointment
For more than one problem.
We don't like to keep people waiting.'

His pen twitched nervously
Above the paper
Ready to plunge.
Before I could form my words
My mother spoke,
'I don't know why I'm here
Haven't been ill for years.
Well, you know that, Doctor,
You didn't even recognise me.'
Her timing was uncanny
As I knew she could not hear.

I cleared my throat,
'We're worried
That our mother
Struggles
To remember things…'

'What sort of things?' he asked.
So I began,
Mindful of the ticking clock,
'Forgets to have a bath
To lock the door
To eat enough
To drink at all…'

'What I detest,' my mother said
'Is people talking about me
As if I am not here!'

More Than One Problem

Knowing that my mother's cognitive skills were declining more rapidly, I decided to book a consultation with her doctor. My mother did not previously have long term health issues and neither was she on any prescribed medication. Therefore, she hardly ever visited the doctor and was proud of what she called her 'rude health'.

As my mother did not recognise that she needed help, to encourage her to attend I had to be less than honest, telling her she had been called in for a check-up.

We have taken my mother to numerous appointments over the last few years and this was one of the most unsatisfactory. In fairness to the doctor, he was trying to address a complex issue in ten minutes, hence the way his eyes 'Flicked up to the clock'. My mother's denial that there was anything wrong, coupled with her deafness, made effective communication almost impossible. While attempting to describe her changing behaviour, I was frustrated by these constraints.

In addition, I felt disloyal when revealing personal information about my mother because she did not realise what was being said. However, had she been included in the conversation, she would have continued to deny that her behaviour had changed or that there was anything wrong with her. Nonetheless, I could empathise with my mother's standpoint; she was aware of being discussed and felt shut out of the conversation. Generally, this is considered to be poor practice.

In this poem, I have tried to portray how unsatisfactory the whole situation was. Finishing with my mother's outburst emphasises the frustrating lack of progress. The reader becomes aware that the appointment is nearly over and yet nothing constructive has been achieved.

Knowing

Scans of Mother's brain
Confirmed what her children already knew
Or guessed, at least.

Evidence of mini strokes and
Vascular, Alzheimer's
Or a lavish double dose.

More resigned than surprised,
We thought back
Over months and years,
Reviewed each certain sign of her decline.

With diagnosis
Would we know a plan
For the way ahead?
'This medication sometimes helps,'
They said.

Fearful of disclosing
To Mother
What we knew of her disease,
We imagined anger or despair
But instead
She seemed unbothered,

As if the message
Never reached her brain
Though we tried to send it
Time and again.

With feisty independence
She sealed the medication
Within an envelope
And scrawled this note upon the front,
(For whom?)
'I haven't been ill since I was twelve
With German measles,
So I don't need medicine.
Surely I would know if I was ILL!'
Eventually we found this
Buried in her kitchen bin.

Knowing

The theme of knowledge often seems central to discussions about dementia and this poem focusses on revelation and concealment. Carers often notice that the person with dementia is unlearning things, such as how to unlock a door or how to open an envelope. There is also much sadness when someone loses knowledge about people they have been close to, forgetting names, personal history and even misunderstanding the nature of their relationship with someone else. So, for example, a son becomes known as a brother or a daughter is believed to be a member of staff or perhaps a stranger.

When my mother was diagnosed with dementia, she did not understand or accept that she had the disease. It was as if the part of her brain which might have acknowledged it had already closed down. It seems strange to me that she did not generally appear to notice what faculties she was beginning to lose. If she did notice, she tried to hide this from us and maybe also from herself. For example, she would tell us that the back door key was lost so she could not spend time in the garden. The key was actually in the lock but she had probably forgotten how to use it.

Not acknowledging that she had dementia, meant that my mother did not comply with the various strategies her offspring tried to put in place to help her continue living at home. She knew she wanted to remain totally independent but did not appreciate that this was no longer possible. Her feistiness regarding the medication, as mentioned here, is one example of this gap in understanding.

The poem also refers to the guilt which can be experienced by carers as they try to impart information, to be honest with the person who has dementia. There are times when honesty does not seem adequate or appropriate.

"Dear children, let us not love with words or speech but with actions and in truth."
(1 John 3:18)

Birthday
It's my birthday today.
Ninety years old.
I know I sound like Eeyore
But I haven't seen a soul.
Waited here all day
No point in getting dressed.
No cards, no phone calls either.
Just me and the cat
Celebrating on our own
With a cake from the cupboard
And a pot of tea.
I expect my family
All have better things to do.
I don't think anyone gives a damn
How old I am!

I suppose they would all
Come running
In some dire emergency –
God forbid –
But just spend time
With me
Enjoying ourselves?
Not likely!

Birthday

At first, the reader will probably feel huge sympathy for the narrator. She is bemoaning the lack of company and support which she receives from her family. She relates how she has just spent her ninetieth birthday with only her cat for company.

The line, 'No point in getting dressed,' could be seen as a reference to my mother being depressed. By this time, she was spending most of the day in bed and took little interest in changing out of her night clothes, unless one of us arrived to take her out. This was partly due to a lack of energy but also because she was finding it harder to dress herself independently, in spite of our efforts to organise her clothes and make them more accessible.

This poem is based on a letter which I discovered in my mother's kitchen, ready to be posted. She had written it to a friend who had turned ninety some months before. When I found the letter, it was still a year and a week until my mother's ninetieth birthday. Reading it stirred up mixed emotions. While I was irritated at the false accusations, I also felt sad that my mother now had so little trust in her family and felt betrayed by them. In her confusion, she would genuinely have felt distraught, even though she did not need to, and I was sorry for this too.

Often, those with dementia misunderstand things, or have delusions and even paranoia. Those who care for them may be quick to reassure, once they are aware of this reality gap. However, in the meantime, the person with dementia may have suffered from extreme negative emotions as a result. The intensity and endurance of these emotions can become a further obstacle to maintaining relationships based on love and trust.

You Just Have To Laugh

Sometimes you just have to laugh
To help you through.

In the early days
We shared amusing anecdotes
Like excited, delighted children
Swapping football cards at break.

Mounds of marshmallows
In Mother's cluttered kitchen
Everywhere you looked.
Was sweet rationing to return?
She ate marmalade
Like chocolate mousse -
A pot swallowed in one meal.
A cat not ill but definitely dead.
The incredible shrinking bath
And a kettle which kept on growing.
Loud party music late at night.
A visit from her aunt.
Countless sealed envelopes
Of buttons, staples, string
Or anything

Which needed to be sorted,
Their contents scribbled on the front.

She labelled photographs
With random family names
Rather than leave them blank
And wrote a fountain
Of dynamic letters
We felt guilty intercepting.
Mother warned a grand-daughter
Against her chosen occupation –
Becoming a long-distance
Lorry driver.
She sent career advice
To Number 10,
Security tips to The Louvre
And fond greetings to all
Residents of Urbino.
These in fluent Italian.

But always,
Behind our smiles and laughs
Worry lay waiting in the wings,
Unvoiced questions
We did not yet share.

You Just Have To Laugh

Spending time with my mother during her illness has not always been dispiriting. Often, her funny comments have lightened the mood and reminded us of the vivacious person she used to be. In the early days of her dementia, her family enjoyed sharing 'amusing anecdotes' about Mother's increasingly strange behaviour. This rich vein has provided all the examples given here. The simile about 'swapping football cards' implies a lack of responsibility, as well as highlighting the idea of fun. There is a suggestion too that this activity may be inappropriate; yet it seems pragmatic, as humour is a good way of helping people through difficult times.

Some aspects of my mother's behaviour were perplexing as well as amusing. She was delusional about her bath having become smaller since she moved into her house, claiming it had been swapped for a three-quarter size bath which was too small for her needs. Also, she believed that her kettle had increased in size, maybe because she was struggling to use it.

My mother always used to love writing, whether it was non-fiction, autobiographical works, poetry, lecture notes, or a myriad of letters to all and sundry. This essential trait has been one of the last to disappear. The fourth stanza explains how her joy of writing manifested itself during the middle stages of dementia. As Mother's memory became more confused, we often received several, almost identical, letters over the course of a few days. She also had the habit of adding reams of notes on the outside of the envelope – usually repeating what was already written inside. Visiting our mother, we would scout around for any letters not yet posted and decide which could escape censorship. Although we felt 'guilty intercepting', this was often necessary to prevent her from upsetting other people.

The final stanza is more sombre in mood, as we are reminded of the reality beneath the surface, where 'Behind our smiles and laughs / Worry lay waiting in the wings'. There is also a hint of further changes ahead, in the lines, 'Unvoiced questions / We did not yet share'. Here we have a sense that the fun is soon to end.

Home Visits

As I began to turn the key,
I never knew
What to expect
Or how to be prepared.
I had to discover
A strange species of courage.

Late morning, but
She might still be in bed -
Despite the carer's efforts -
The duvet hooding over head.
Unaware of time or place
Or the bitter, choking stench
Which suffused the cluttered room.

If she slept on,
I could creep around her
Cautiously,
Sifting post and scribbled notes,
Mopping floors,
Remove half-eaten meals
And drinks congealed.

Better sleeping yet
Than perched

Like some scrawny, balding chicken
Uncomfortable
Confused
Waiting
Trembling
Half-dressed.

When she noticed me,
Which often took a while,
A faint but welcome smile would
Curve across her pale face.
On a good day she would
Excuse her idleness,
Accept my help
Too readily.

Though feeling disempowered,
I tried to hide concern from her,
Burying it within
The grainy layer of chores.
Things were
Unsatisfactory at best.

Home Visits

I wrote this poem long after my mother went into a care home, while I was reflecting on how much more difficult it had been for all her carers when she was still living in her own home. The poem describes how things were during the middle stages of my mother's disease. I was feeling overwhelmed at times, suddenly sharing accountability for my mother's welfare and yet unprepared for this duty. As she was so unaware of her changing behaviour and her limitations, the burden of responsibility seemed even greater.

There were feelings of guilt too. 'Sifting post and scribbled notes' could be viewed as an invasion of my mother's privacy, a way of denying her right to communicate with others. However, to protect her reputation and the sensitivities of others, this needed to be done.

When I used to see a stranger looking neglected, dirty and uncared for, I would find it hard to stifle negative feelings of judgement towards that person and their family. How could people live like this? Did nobody care? Seeing my mother in this 'neglected' state, despite our best efforts to support her while living in her own home, made me re-evaluate. I was also acutely aware that others might be judging us. This reminded me of these verses in Matthew,

"Do not judge, or you too will be judged. For in the same way you judge others, you will be judged, and with the measure you use, it will be measured to you. Why do you look at the speck of sawdust in your brother's eye and pay no attention to the plank in your own eye? How can you say to your brother, 'Let me take the speck out of your eye,' when all the time there is a plank in your own eye?" (Matthew 7: 1-4)

One indication of my mother's decline was that she would often 'Accept my help / Too readily.' She had been so fiercely independent for most of her life and would still sometimes be aggressive towards the care staff who visited her. As the dementia progressed, this level of care proved to be inadequate and 'Unsatisfactory at best.'

Water Resistant

Mother told us, many times,
How she learned to swim
In the River Avon,
Icy cold even in summer
Chilling but thrilling.
And seaside trips
Demanded several swims
Hobbling over pebbles
Through the shallows
To splash over surf
And out of her depth
Where she loved to be.

So now it seems strange to see
Her fervently avoiding water,
Resisting baths or showers,
Declining drinks
As if she is no longer waterproof
And fears she might become
Nothing but a mushy pulp
Like tissue remnants from the wash.

Water Resistant

There is a paradox central to this poem - how my mother's love of water mutated into a fear of it. The sharp contrast between these emotions highlights how dementia can appear to rob a person of aspects of their personality that used to be so fundamental.

We have clear memories of how this person used to be, before dementia. Even some of their frustrating qualities are remembered fondly because this was their true identity. So, for example, my mother used to be infatuated with swimming in the sea; hence the lines, 'And seaside trips / Demanded several swims'. She loved the sense of freedom and rebellion, especially going far out of her depth to leave everyone else behind, on or near the shore. Continuing to swim in the sea well into her eighties, she did not understand why her friends were not similarly enamoured with the idea.

Becoming 'resistant' to water crept in gradually for my mother. Early on in the illness, her offspring noticed that she was not keeping herself clean like she used to. Everyday habits, such as cleaning her teeth, became regarded as too much of a chore and then were forgotten. It is sad to see people close to you neglecting themselves like this.

My mother used to enjoy several cups of tea, coffee and squash each day as well as the occasional sherry or glass of cider. As her dementia has progressed, she has been reluctant to drink at all and needs much prompting. There is evidence linking dehydration with an increased risk of confusion and disorientation in people with dementia. As the illness progresses, they lose the ability to feel thirsty.

In her care home, my mother has been given showers and later bed baths, sometimes much to her annoyance. She has been generally comfortable, lying day and night in a warm bed, and often resented being disturbed. Sometimes she has seemed genuinely frightened. Asked to wait in the corridor, I could hear her shouting angrily at the care staff, which seemed quite out of character.

Leave Me Alone
In many ways
She was already alone,
Stretched out under the sheets
Sculpted by the previous visitor,
Separated from the commotion
Around her,
Quiet and
Almost motionless
Only her fingers twitching on the soft blanket,
Perhaps a quest for human touch
But comfortable for now.

In her dreams she could jump the waves,
Climb the rocks and wave the victory flag
While others watched from down below.

Two figures, one each side of the lofty bed
One held her hand,
The other moved her leg.
Who were these strangers in her way?
'Leave me alone!' she cried.

Leave Me Alone

Dementia interrupts communication between people, making it harder to sustain good relationships. Many of those with the illness become increasingly isolated from family and friends and often feel lonely.

In my mother's case, loneliness was made worse by the extreme deafness which she failed to acknowledge. Long before she developed dementia, she had been prescribed with a hearing aid, wore it once or twice and then abandoned it because it gave her a headache. It is possible that her hearing loss was a risk factor for dementia; it certainly worsened the symptoms and made helping her more difficult. For many years, as well as facing my mother so that she could lip-read, I have written down everything I am telling her. Sometimes, she used to try to write back to me - a sign of misunderstanding.

With severe hearing loss and following many house moves, my mother lost touch with virtually all her friends by the time she went to live in a care home. She was unable to make new friends either; our hopes that she might become more sociable and interactive in the care home were to be disappointed.

This poem describes how separate my mother has seemed from her environment, towards the end of her life. There is only a vague connection, as she touches the blanket in 'Perhaps a quest for human touch'. This contrasts with her exasperation, in the final verse, with the 'strangers' who are trying to give her personal care.

On a more positive note, I imagined the dreams my mother might be experiencing. Here is her former self, active and adventurous. Instead of being like an object controlled by others, she is dominant and free. On many occasions, she has seemed happier asleep than awake which has made me reluctant to rouse her.

Dream Time

Does my mother dream of the times
Before she knew me
And were things really better then?

Does she dream
Of leaping over waves
Pitching her tent by the woods
And collecting sticks for camp fires?

Are the pictures clear?
And, in her dreams, is her mind refreshed?
Does her conversation flow?
Can she recall the names
And stories
Of those she meets
And the realms she visits?

Or are her dreams nothing more
Than fuzzy, flickering feelings of
Wonder, joy and peace?

Dream Time

This poem continues to explore the theme of dreams. The title refers to the Aboriginal belief that the world was created by their ancestors back in the very beginning of time, the Dream Time. I chose the title to reflect the idea that dreams can be creative and prophetic, in addition to being a way of processing life's experiences.

I wrote the poem after my husband asked, 'What do you think your mother dreams about?' when she had advanced dementia and was sleeping very soundly for almost all the time.

Those with dementia usually find it easier to remember events from long ago as these are now in their long-term memory, having been reprocessed many times. I included some of the happiest experiences my mother had previously related about her childhood, thinking she would be likely to recall these still. It cheered me to believe that she could continue to have good experiences, if only just in dreams. Even if my mother could only dream with 'fuzzy, flickering feelings', this was a positive.

While writing the final stanzas, I became more aware of the healing power of dreams and their connection with the supernatural world beyond our normal experience. I was mindful too of the exciting promise of new bodies given in the Bible.

"So will it be with the resurrection of the dead. The body that is sown is perishable, it is raised imperishable; it is sown in dishonour, it is raised in glory; it is sown in weakness, it is raised in power; it is sown a natural body, it is raised a spiritual body."

(1 Corinthians 15: 42-44)

Who Are You?

I am the soft, mumbling voice
And the blurred shadow before your eyes.

I am the fresh scent of country air
Drifting through the open window,

The lightest touch upon your hand
And the sweetness of soft marzipan
Upon your tongue.

We hold hands across the decades
Of delights, disappointments and disasters,
Each relishing, recalling and regretting
But no longer able to share.

Who Are You?

The interrogative title of 'Who Are You?' highlights the theme of identity. I imagined my mother asking herself this question (as she became vaguely aware of my presence in her room) and then seeking to answer it. Several friends have asked me whether my mother 'knows' who I am. They are surprised when I respond by saying that she sometimes still uses my name and that I have heard her introduce me to staff as her daughter. Yet, in many ways, she no longer knows me; her knowledge of my life is based mostly on information she gathered years, or even decades ago.

When children are being taught to write poetry, they are often encouraged to refer to different senses so that their writing becomes more vivid. Aware that my mother, with advanced dementia, could barely use her senses to interpret the diminishing world around her, I wrote this poem to imagine the fragments of her senses which might remain.

I tried to focus on the ways in which my mother could still perceive my presence. This led to a review of our turbulent relationship, from my point of view as well as hers, hence the phrases, 'delights, disappointments and disasters' and the echoing ideas of 'relishing, recalling and regretting'.

There is an understated frustration in the final line, as communication has become difficult and limited. However, holding hands is seen as a symbol of love and a lasting connection.

"Be kind and compassionate to one another, forgiving each other, just as in Christ God forgave you."

(Ephesians 4:32)

The Lights Are Too Bright.
The lights are too bright.
Why don't they switch them off?
Just want to sleep now. Feel so tired.
Never been so tired.
Such a comfortable bed.
Just right for sleeping.
But the lights are too bright.
They should turn them off…

A happy dream just then
At the seaside.
Mother and brother and friend.
Now, what were their names?
Never mind. Doesn't really matter.
Playing in those little lakes.
The ones the sea leaves behind.
What are they called?
Oh, doesn't really matter.
Cold and dark. But animals live there.
Hiding.
Splash!
Here's one. Look!
Caught one.
Watch out. Might bite.

Much too bright these lights.
Shouldn't be on.
It's the middle of the night. Midnight.
Who's that? Don't touch me.
Leave me alone!
Let me sleep.
Here's a fork in my hand.
Doesn't look like food. Mush.
Not hungry. Don't want it.
Give it to the cat!
I want to sleep now.
It's been a long day…

I know that face. That's my daughter.
She's grown up quickly.
Looks sad. Not sure why.
She shows some old pictures.
That's you, she says.
Well, I know that!
Feel so tired.
She's still talking. And pointing.
But the pictures are all mush.
Fuzzy. Can't see them.
So tired.
Just need a bit of sleep.
Then I'll feel better.

The Lights Are Too Bright

To gain greater empathy for her, I gave my mother the narrative voice in this poem. The events described occur over the course of a morning, despite her belief that 'It's the middle of the night'. I have attempted to show how she interprets or misinterprets what is happening in her room.

It has become one of my mother's habits, in the advanced stages of dementia, to complain about the lights being too bright; I think that this results from extreme fatigue and her desire to sleep for almost all the time. Certainly, she has had little concept of day or night for a couple of years now. Ironically, carers are advised to make sure rooms are well lit, so that the person with dementia can find things easily and be less inclined to misinterpret their surroundings.

The limited vocabulary and short, disjointed phrases and sentences included here were chosen to reflect my mother's erratic thought patterns and memory loss. I have also featured some phrases which have recently become habitual, such as 'Leave me alone!', 'Let me sleep.' and 'Doesn't really matter' as well as some favourite sayings from before she developed dementia, like 'Well, I know that' and 'Give it to the cat'. These remnants of her past life suggest that the essence of her personality is still there under the surface.

"Every good and perfect gift is from above, coming down from the Father of the heavenly lights, who does not change like shifting shadows."

(James 1:17)

Thinking...Thinking
Well, I may be vague at times
But nowhere near as muddled
As my Granny was,
Whatever she was called.

Now I have been jumped on by my cat.
Quite a weight.
A he or a she? Let's call him Natasha –
I definitely had a cat called that.
She paws at the blanket
Then tries to burrow beneath the duvet
So I ask her, as sternly as I can,
'Whose bed is it anyway?'
But she does not reply.

Living here is alright, I suppose
Though rather lonely from time to time.
Still, better to be on your own
Than with the wrong person.
At least I have learnt that from life.

I could do with a friend or three.
What about that retired architect
My daughter said she knew?
It has to be someone
Who genuinely shares

At least one of my interests.
And the Welsh have an extra language
Which never seems quite fair.
So probably not anyone Welsh.

Well, I continue
In my usual rude health.
Of course I am keeping myself well –
Not much point doing anything else.
I may have said that before.

I'm letting the garden look after itself.
There are jolly cards up on the shelf.
I have been spoilt rotten.
What have I done to deserve them?
I might be a whole year older
Maybe getting on in years
But I can't really help that, can I?
I might last another year or two
Then they could get
Fed up with me. We shall see.

Thinking...Thinking

This poem aims to demonstrate the disjointed thinking created by dementia and the way in which connections to reality become more fragile. This is why my mother claims to be less 'muddled' than her own grandmother and why her cat seems to change gender within the line, 'Let's call him Natasha.'

I have included several of my mother's actual comments. Some of these have been favourite sayings for decades, such as 'Still, better to be on your own / Than with the wrong person.' Topics in the poem are not completely random, however; each indicates a strong emotion or motivation and there are tenuous links between them. So, for example, my mother's interest in her cat leads on to her considering her loneliness and what sort of friend she might think worth cultivating.

As a carer, I have often scrutinised my mother's comments. I have learnt to look beneath the surface to understand the wider context from these random and often seemingly trivial vestiges of communication. Sometimes, by analysing in this way, it has been possible to gauge my mother's emotions and allay worries which were less evident.

The final four lines of the poem are based on a scribbled note which I found, written by my mother when she was still living in her own home. These lines may seem shocking in contrast to the rather whimsical tone of the remainder of the poem. Indeed, I was shocked when I first read them. This was the only time in decades that I had heard my mother acknowledge her mortality. Also, I felt justly accused and ashamed on reading the words, 'they could get fed up with me'. This idea left me feeling most uncomfortable.

A Thief In The Night
It sneaked in like a thief in the night,
Unopposed, unnoticed, unheard.
Did someone forget to bolt the door?
Had a window been left ajar?

Dementia rifled through
Mother's cupboards and cases,
Plundered memories and dreams,
Disturbing any order,
Leaving chaos in its wake.

The owner felt bemused;
She could not remember saying,
Come in and help yourself.'

Mother sat still amid the turmoil,
Defeated and her ego bruised
But unsure what had gone before.
While others made lists of losses
And unsuccessful claims,
She sought to ask,
'What is all the fuss about?'
But these words were missing too.

A Thief In The Night

I chose to personify dementia as a thief to emphasise the shock and anger which many people experience, as dementia begins to disrupt the life of a person who is close to them. In this poem, the 'owner' or person with dementia is also shocked but experiences confusion rather than anger. There is ambiguity in the words, 'unsure what has gone before' which reflects my mother's sense of bewilderment.

At the end of the poem, we learn that even her words have gone 'missing' so she is unable to express herself, to ask a question and to have help solving the mystery. People with dementia often become frustrated as they struggle to formulate sentences and make their feelings known.

By using personification, I found it easier to express anger about my mother's declining faculties. It feels better having someone to blame. Alhough the title was suggested by the verses from Matthew, where a 'thief in the night' becomes a simile for unpredictability, the 'thief' in my poem is not good (like Jesus) but malevolent and underhand. There are times when it is difficult to be anything but despondent about dementia and the mood of this poem reflects this.

"Therefore keep watch, because you do not know on what day your Lord will come. But understand this: If the owner of the house had known at what time of night the thief was coming, he would have kept watch and would not have let his house be broken into."

(Matthew 24: 42-43)

Looking For Signs

We stand guard at her bedside
Looking for signs.
She let someone paint her nails,
She's waking up,
She used my name,
She recognised her child self
In that faded photograph.
That's good.

Peering through paperwork
We find further clues,
She ate half her breakfast
The day before yesterday
And some of her jelly last night.
But the full, neglected beakers
Stare at us accusingly
Like sentries,
As if to say
You can look for signs,
But are they signs of life?

Looking For Signs

'Looking for Signs' is written from the family's point of view, as they survey the person with dementia and her room in order to gauge the progress of the disease and her general health. Sometimes, my siblings and I have felt like detectives sifting through clues and trying to make sense of a mystery.

In the first line, I have used the term, 'stand guard' and later the lines, 'Stare at us accusingly / Like sentries' add to the military analogy. This gives a suggestion of conflict but also emphasises the more objective stance we sometimes need to adopt, when normal communication is no longer possible.

I wrote this when my mother was very ill and there is an unvoiced question which seems to hang in the air: 'How long will she live?' Nobody knows, which is why we look 'for signs'. This idea of progression creates a sense of optimism for much of the poem but the mood becomes more negative before the end, where the 'full, neglected beakers' - with their connotation of dehydration - are portrayed as a threat or even an enemy force. The rhetorical question which completes the poem would probably be left unspoken in real life and yet it would pervade people's thoughts.

"And the peace of God, which transcends all understanding, will guard your hearts and your minds in Christ Jesus."

(Philippians 4:7)

Mother Asleep

Your face framed by bedding,
Eyes firmly closed,
Lavender and borage blue
Like old bruises from a fight forgotten,
Or the marble eyes
Of a baby bird born too soon.
Your face once so familiar,
Now stranger – glimpsing the unknown.

Suppleness and gentle folds
Have surrendered to sharp angles
Bones protruding,
Your skull almost visible
Beneath your tracing paper skin.
Your face once so familiar,
Now stranger – glimpsing the unknown.

Mother Asleep

This was written when my mother was very ill and had been rushed to hospital, having contracted pneumonia with sepsis. We thought it was unlikely that she would survive more than a day or so but she recovered and returned to her care home.

The poem highlights how an elderly person's appearance can change dramatically towards the end of their life. Some of the imagery is shocking; my mother's eyes are compared to bruises or the eyes of an embryonic bird, bones are 'protruding' and her skin is compared to 'tracing paper'. This stark imagery reflects the shock I felt when seeing her like this, compared to my memories of her in good health with her 'suppleness and gentle folds'.

Repetition of the lines, 'Your face once so familiar / Now stranger - glimpsing the unknown' emphasises the idea that my mother is near a gateway into another world. The word 'stranger' is ambiguous; it can be read as a comparative adjective ('more strange') or a noun ('outsider') and both meanings are equally valid in this context.

"Even to your old age and gray hairs
I am he who will sustain you
I have made you and I will carry you
I will sustain you and rescue you."

(Isaiah 46:4)

Turn Off The Lights
Lying there,
Paper thin among the paper sheets
Hand over her eyes,
And wincing from the brightness,
My mother moans,
'Turn off the lights.
Too bright. Too bright.'

Now she prefers the shady places,
Crepuscular realms,
Dreams with dancing, dappled figures
From the past
We cannot see.
Though ethereal and fragile,
This is the world she now prefers.

Turn Off The Lights

Although this poem shares the same theme as 'The Lights are Too Bright', it is written from my point of view, rather than my mother's. Her illness has presented us with many paradoxes and posed many conundrums. Here, I focus on my effort to comprehend her avoidance of light. While in bed at her care home, she will often complain about the ceiling lights being on. Perhaps she thinks they might stop her sleeping, as they are right in her line of sight. To reinforce the idea of day and night, the care staff turn on the lights at breakfast time unless it is particularly bright outside.

My mother used to love brightness and colour; some of her favourite times were sunny days among Greek ruins or playing at the beach, so her new preference for 'crepuscular realms' has been a clear indication of change and loss. She wrote two books about stained glass and used to enthuse about the way natural light brought the windows to life. When giving lectures, she would show particular admiration for artists, such as Caravaggio or Constable, who used light to create dramatic effects within their paintings.

The end of the poem suggests that she prefers her dream world, for this is where she can feel alive and bright, with 'the dancing, dappled figures'. However, this is not a world which can be shared with others, adding to the idea of disconnectedness. The words 'ethereal and fragile' echo the description of my mother's appearance at the start of the poem, where she is described as 'paper thin'. This emphasises her extreme frailty.

"Even though I walk through the valley of the shadow of death, I will fear no evil, for you are with me; your rod and your staff, they comfort me."

(Psalm 23:1-4)

In The Care Home

Here it is warm but airless
Like a departure lounge,
Cocooned from the breezes outside,
Part of this world, yet
Apart from this world.
This staging post -
A lay-by beside the highway
Beneath the steamy August sun.

The floor glows
Expectantly.
The décor is bright but bland
And the smell of disinfectant infuses us
Like embalming fluid,
Preserving the appearance of life.

A little agitated now,
My mother trawls the walls for messages
But finds only pictures
Vaguely familiar.
We both await instructions,
Looking for love
In this suffocating warmth.

In The Care Home

So much of modern life involves rushing around, being busy. Caring for someone with dementia offers a strange antidote to this.

For me, apart from the occasional crisis, most visiting times have seemed peaceful but also protracted and often tedious. While my mother has been awake, I have communicated with her by writing things down - necessary due to her extreme deafness. This is a slow process which often appears to be a waste of time, as she only occasionally responds appropriately. I have to keep trying though, in the hope that we can still maintain some sort of beneficial connection.

This poem attempts to portray the claustrophobic atmosphere of my mother's bedroom in the care home. It is clean, safe and warm, providing for all her physical needs. However, it does not have the permanence of 'home' but feels more like a staging post on a journey. There is a sense that she is looking back, in the lines, 'But finds only pictures / Vaguely familiar' as well as forward; the theme of waiting on a frontier between two worlds pervades the whole poem.

The second verse alludes to death in the reference to embalming fluid. It is perhaps this thought which makes my mother 'agitated'. She is searching the walls 'for messages', some reassurance of her destination - like someone reading the monitors in the departure lounge. 'Looking for love' is deliberately ambiguous, referring to my relationship with my mother and our search for comfort from God.

Letting Go

My mother lies motionless
Tucked up tightly like a young baby
Beneath soft sheets and a thin blanket.
She mumbles something
About putting out milk bottles.
We count the years, months, weeks
And days of decline.
So long since
So long.

She clutches at the blanket now
Fingers strained, white at the tips,

While we hold those moments
Until the moments become memories.
None of us find it easy
Letting go.

Letting Go

'Letting Go' explores different ways in which we try to hold on, or struggle to let go, towards the end of life.

Somewhere in my mother's mind there still remained the burden of responsibility for household chores, such as leaving out the bottles for the milkman. There is a touch of humorous irony here, as we see her hardly able to move, almost helpless 'like a young baby'. Carers often say that people with dementia become more like young children, yet in some ways this comparison is incongruous. While children make progress as time passes, those with dementia regress. The way in which my mother grasps her blanket so firmly symbolises her reluctance to let go of life itself.

Sometimes, when we are caring for someone with dementia, we feel powerless to help them. During my mother's illness, I have had plenty of time to consider the progression of her dementia, 'the years, months, weeks / And days of decline'. I have tried to express a sense of regret and resignation in the lines, 'So long since / So long.'

While accepting that my mother's quality of life is poor, I also struggle to imagine letting her go completely as I contemplate her approaching death. The comfort here is that the 'moments become memories'; thus there is transformation and nothing needs to be completely lost for ever.

"There is no fear in love. But perfect love drives out fear, because fear has to do with punishment. The one who fears is not made perfect in love."

(1 John 4:18)

Low Tide

We lean heavily on limpets
To peer into the pool,
Looking for signs of life below the surface
Of that stewed sea-water soup,
A brimming bowl.
How can we fathom its murky depths?

In her lofty bed
My mother stirs.
We hear her quip
An unexpected drop of essence
Into our solemn conversation.
A sliver of light darts across
Like a needle through sacking.
One small fish
Abandoned by the receding tide –
Remnant of a gleaming shoal.

As hours drift
We watch and wait
To welcome a return.
But now the brine congeals
To an oily mirror.

Those unforgiving limpets
Have imprinted our palms.

Less earnest now,
We resent the numbness,
Rubbing our hands wildly
To restore feeling.

Low Tide

My mother used to love spending time at the seaside. Childhood photographs show her in Dorset, Devon, Cornwall and Jersey, playing, paddling, swimming and splashing around in a strange little boat which her family called 'The Tadpole'. During the Second World War, when she was a teenager, my mother hugely resented the fact that the beaches were cordoned off with barbed wire and access denied.

We could also tell how much she loved the sea as an adult. There are photographs of her doing handstands and cartwheels in the sand on honeymoon, for example. When I was a child, our summer holidays were almost always beach holidays - again in the West Country as well as Ireland and France. Mother would seem more like a child at times, excitedly clambering over rocks and exploring the pools with her children.

It seemed appropriate to choose a beach setting to provide the background for this poem, as it concerns the essence of my mother's personality, the 'remnant of a gleaming shoal'. The rock pool represents my mother's life now. With advanced dementia, her mind is unclear, like 'stewed sea-water soup', and those who spend time with her find it hard to understand her thought patterns and her behaviour.

Suddenly, there is delight and shock as my mother has a moment of clarity, saying something clever, succinct and appropriate. Her family hope for more but that is all, just a moment. Losing patience, her family recall the pain they have suffered, 'Those unforgiving limpets / Have imprinted our palms' and focus on that. However, we have glimpsed and remembered the person whom she used to be: an author and lecturer, a lover of words and word play.

Thursday's Child

When I was only two or three
Which would have been round 1930
My mother sometimes said to me,
'Thursday's child has far to go.'
Taking no time to fathom this out,
I would wriggle from her embrace
And wildly race across the lawn
Towards the sand pit – my personal beach
I loved it there, far out of reach.

I attended to my father's tales-
Always the lone explorer,
No witness to endorse his claims
But captivating nonetheless.
Yearning to start those grand adventures,
To declare them as my own,
I quickly learned to swim,
To ride my brother's bike
And sprinted faster than the boys,
My name engraved upon the cup.

My husbands and my children
Held me back, of course.
How often did I want to charge away,
Kick my heels and toss my chestnut hair,
Throw caution to the wind,

Get out of there?
But births like brakes
And chores like chocks
Prevented me from taking off,
My lover's pleas denied.

The empty nest for me
At last meant liberty
To choose, to go or stay.
Nothing quite like moving house
To lighten up my way.
Seven perfect places
Where the dust did not settle
Or at least I saw none.

So here I am.
I have arrived
Like the Queen of Sheba
(Though with far less noise and fuss).
I have attained this royal bed
A high and mighty place.
I have come so far
And yet
Still know I have so far to go.

Thursday's Child

'Thursday's Child' could be read as a potted biography of my mother, from her lively toddler days to the present. It serves as a salutary reminder that an emphasis on life-history is significant in understanding and caring for those with dementia. When people with dementia are able to share their life stories, it enhances their sense of identity and self-esteem. Those who look after them are able to develop more positive and person-centred care.

Beneath the biographical details, there is an undercurrent of irony. My mother's view of her life - long before she developed dementia - has often seemed distorted to me. Though understandably proud of many achievements, she has rarely admitted to making mistakes. Much has been exaggerated to create a better story and some episodes completely rewritten to put her in a more positive light.

While the first two stanzas aim to offer a fair account of my mother's motivations and achievements, certain later lines of the poem give only half-truths. We learn that,' My husbands and my children / Held me back' and 'The empty nest for me / At last meant liberty'. While it is true that she had a penchant for moving house, her homes were not 'perfect places', although she tried to convince herself that they were.

The final verse brings us to the present day. There is a marked contrast between the hyperactivity of the toddler and this recent dormancy. In her state of confusion, but also as a nod to her long-held delusions of grandeur, I conjectured that my mother might believe that she has somehow earned 'this royal bed'. The sense of irony is more heightened here; the reader remembers the central theme of the poem, having 'far to go', yet sees the narrator as inactive.

However, on another level, the narrator may be correct. As she looks to the future, 'I have so far to go', she could be alluding to her hopes of an afterlife, the journey stretching ahead of her.

Your Hands
Your hands, so skilful then,
Could tie a bow in a heartbeat
Cut the toughest carrots
Hold buttercups beneath my chin
Swing me above the waves,
Brush gold leaf upon a frame
Write fine italics
Prune the wild, rambling rose
Conjure up a landscape,
Use a camera with ease
Sew the finest, neatest hem
Squeeze icing on a birthday cake
Splash whitewash on the walls,

Now, even your hands are weak.
So fragile,
I cradle them gently like baby birds,
Willing you to wake.

Your Hands

I wrote this poem to make myself remember some of the best things which my mother did. In deliberately focussing on the good, it helped me feel less despondent about the ways in which our relationship had been damaged. Also, I became less overwhelmed by the severity of her dementia.

My mother was very good with her hands and I could choose from many examples to illustrate this. Some of these, such as how she would 'hold buttercups beneath my chin' and 'squeeze icing on a birthday cake', are personal to me. Although these behaviours were not as impressive as being able to restore picture frames or do fine watercolour paintings and calligraphy, they were ways in which my mother could show me her love. Often, as I was growing up, I longed to see more of this personal connection and less of the magnificent, public face which she was so keen to promote.

The second stanza offers a stark contrast to the first, as the reader is transported back to the present. Now my mother's hands are weak, whereas they used to be strong and capable. The simile, 'like baby birds', emphasises their fragility. Here, I am able to show love to my mother, even if only by holding hands while she sleeps, and our roles are reversed. On many occasions, when I have visited her, she has been so drowsy that this is the only connection we have. However, it is still an important way of demonstrating forgiveness.

"For we are God's handiwork, created in Christ Jesus to do good works, which God prepared in advance for us to do."

(Ephesians 2:10)

Waiting For The Inevitable
Mother clings to life
With frail fingers,
Her appetite and frame diminished
She is hardly recognisable now.
Lying there asleep and almost still,
Eyes firmly shut, mouth gaping wide.

A light breeze puffs at the curtain,
The television chatters on
Yet still she sleeps, oblivious,
Not knowing where she lies
And no idea she's even ill.
'It's just a matter of waiting…'
Said the carer gently,
'Waiting for the inevitable.'

Death feels so close now,
It hovers over her.
Beneath the whirring blades
You can almost hear the scratching of nails
And the patter of small stones
Crumbling from the edge of the cliff.
But then again, perhaps she's stronger
Than she looks. Who knows?

Waiting For The Inevitable

One day, a member of staff at my mother's care home commented, 'It's just a matter of waiting, waiting for the inevitable.' At first I accepted this at face value, but later in the day I felt perplexed as I tried to interpret what had been said.

Even when a person with dementia is very ill and frail, those experienced in caring for them are often unable to judge how long they will live. Some people cling on to life, while others seem to have decided that they have had enough. My mother has shown tenacity, which was always a key personality trait. She has never accepted that she had dementia and she has also seemed unaware of her impending death.

The final verse shows my perspective rather than hers. I perceive that death is approaching, yet this awareness is based on incomplete knowledge. Using imagery connected with the potential recovery of a body from the base of a cliff reflects a drama which often remains hidden, the internal struggle between life and death.

Ending the poem with a rhetorical question underlines the dilemma many of us face: how to prepare for death if we do not know when it is coming. It is at moments like this that I ask God to take away my anxiety, trusting he will provide all the help I will need when the time comes.

"My Father's house has many rooms; if that were not so, would I have told you that I am going there to prepare a place for you? And if I go and prepare a place for you, I will come back and take you to be with me that you also may be where I am."

(John 14:2-3)

Remembering

Let us try to remember the good times.
Our bedtime stories, like
'The Cat that Walked by
Himself'-
You admired his independence,
And all those real cats and countless kittens,
And the funny stories about our ancestors –
Your father smuggling
Bird of paradise feathers,
Your dotty grandmother using hymns
To remember
Phone numbers.

There were huge casseroles and
Copious supplies of crumbly scones
With home-made jam,
Sometimes left behind on picnics
But always ultimately enjoyed,
Other than the plum stones.

We were surprised by your sense of fun.
The plastic frog,
Perched on the plug,
Peering out from the bubbled bath,
So lifelike

That we dared not enter
Such dangerous waters,
As no mother would play such a trick.

We shared
Holidays in Devon,
Holidays abroad,
Searching rock pools,
Surprising the limpets,
You showed us how to shrimp
With that enormous net.
You taught me to swim
In the warm, French sea.
We discovered colossal, ancient columns
As we dived in the waters near Corinth.

Let us try to remember
Your endless search for adventure
And new beginnings -
So often the essence
Of good times.
I remember and as I remember
I wonder
What frontiers
You are exploring now.

Remembering

'Remembering' was an attempt to reclaim and cherish some of the good memories which I had of my mother. It was not only the dementia which had made me feel pessimistic; my relationship with her had been difficult for decades. Having written several more melancholy poems about her, I was trying to find some 'beauty in the ashes' to raise my spirits. It also occurred to me that if my mother died soon, I might be so overwhelmed by negative emotions that I would have nothing uplifting to say about her at her funeral, so this gave me added motivation.

The poem represents a celebration of my mother's life, or at least the positive experiences that my siblings and I were able to share with her. I chose to write in the first person plural, to include my sister and two brothers and tried to speak for us all. (I was conscious that some of these special times involved my sister Cathy too. She died after being knocked down by a car, when she was nine and I was four.) However it is interesting, that, although there is much common ground, when we share our memories of our mother we do not always impart the same significance to each habit or behaviour. Our personal experience is unique.

Each stanza focusses on a very different aspect of my mother's personality - her story telling, provision of food, sense of humour, passion for education and finally, her pursuit of adventure.

The end of the poem, 'I wonder / What frontiers / You are exploring now.' alludes to this love of adventure but also emphasises the feelings of strangeness or otherworldliness that dementia can convey. In the final line, I chose the word 'frontiers' to imply that my mother - in spite of her many difficulties - still has an independent, pioneering spirit.

Your Hand In Mine

With your hand in mine,
I can safely bridge the gap
From chair to sofa.

With your hand in mine
I cling anxiously
As we reach the playground
But will be brave for you.

With your hand in mine
We are invincible,
We can sprint over the sands
And leap the lively waves.

With your hand in mine,
Now you stagger against a wall
So I steady you towards the shop.

With your hand in mine
I hold on tenderly
Willing you to wake.

Your Hand In Mine

Other than her head, it is usually only my mother's hands which are visible when I visit her in the care home, so they have become a natural focus for my thoughts. Hands are significant too for their connotations with generosity, communication and hospitality. My mother is in bed all day and night, warm and comfortable for the most part. If she is sleeping soundly, sometimes I hold her hand while quietly praying for her.

Although written entirely in the present tense, to give it a greater sense of immediacy, the poem gives a condensed history of the times when my mother and I have held hands. From seeing me as an unsteady toddler needing my mother's physical help, we then have a snapshot of early childhood when my anxiety at starting school was alleviated by the emotional support she gave me. By the third verse, my mother and I have become more like equals and this is pivotal. The final two verses show a role reversal, whereby she becomes unsteady and needs my physical and emotional support.

Looking back over my relationship with my mother, there have been many, many times when it was tortuous and I wondered if it even had a future. Now that she is so vulnerable, I am learning much about forgiveness. Although there is no point in trying to settle old scores or encourage her to see my truths, I do not want this to make me bitter. She is no longer a threat to me and she cannot add to the 'record of wrongs', so with the help of God, I am learning to choose to be kind and let things go.

"Whatever you did for one of the least of these brothers and sisters of mine, you did for me."

(Matthew 25:40)

Questions
Although she lacks the energy to sit up,
Today my mother sends
A surge of questions
That wash across the room like waves
Breaking on a pebbled shore.
The shifting ground and sound
Unsteady me.

I struggle to respond directly.
My mind begins to float
Freely away
On a wide sea of probabilities
And possibilities,
Beyond the tide,
Beyond the rows of towering waves.
I plunge
But still she pulls me in.
Perhaps the cord has been there all along.
Yet another question
More random than before.
What answer can I give
To calm or to assuage?

I look
Towards the bold yellow wall

Then inwards
For hope and inspiration.
But, looking back.
I find her sound asleep.
No turbulent ocean
But a millpond. No answer is required.

Questions

One day when I was visiting my mother, I was surprised to find her mind so active. She stayed awake for about forty minutes, instead of the usual three or four, asking a series of questions and only repeating herself occasionally. This was most unusual.

She was wondering if she should return to Italy. If so, who would like to accompany her? Would I let her know if I could think of anyone? Then she mentioned drawing and painting, asking me if I thought she should do more of these. She wanted to know if I would like being a bird, as she had decided she would not and did not enjoy flying in planes much either. And so it went on.

This visit gave me an interesting insight into how my mother's mind was working. She would flit from topic to topic and promptly dismiss each idea, in spite of the supportive comments I tried to make. Perhaps this was because she realised that she was unable to plan how to achieve each desire. So, she would mention the distance, the chilly weather or the fact that, although there was nothing wrong with her, she could be 'very lazy.'

One question my mother frequently asked, on this day and at other times too, was 'Can I do anything for you?' It was a sad reminder of the times when she was able to help us and yet my siblings and I found ourselves joking about it later, imagining asking her to help us tile a bathroom or mow the lawn. What motivated her question, however, was a desire to care for us and this sign of love touched my heart.

Connection

What can I offer you now?
Old photographs have been scrutinised
Too much.
They will reveal nothing new
But simply emphasise what you have lost,
Unsettle you.

And pictures on my phone
Lack context, you have told me.
Often your eyes do not even flicker
With recognition.
Grandchildren have become unfamiliar,
Just faces against a background.
What remains to be said?

'Are we going out for lunch?'
You ask brightly,
As if this was even possible.
You have been confined to bed
For at least a year
And the evening shadows are moving in.
'Or are we having something here?'

At this moment
I produce some mint chocolate bubbles
Carefully chosen at the local shop,

Wave the bag with a flourish
Like a baton or a wand.
I offer you one,
Reach towards your outstretched hand.

With surprising pincer grip -
That developmental milestone
Still helps you on your journey -
You pop it in your mouth.
They melt on the tongue,
Which reduces the chance of choking.

The minty tang ignites your eyes;
The sweetness makes you smile.
I smile in return,
You reach for another.
We have found a connection.

Connection

The poem indicates how difficult it can be to sustain a relationship when someone has advanced dementia. Impaired cognitive and communication abilities mean that new strategies need to be sought. At the start of the poem, the narrator feels at a loss as to how to make her visit beneficial; this uncertainty is made clear in the line, 'What remains to be said?' I have often wondered this. On this occasion, before I could say any more, my mother suddenly suggested going out for lunch.

It has been rare for my mother to initiate conversation since she has developed advanced dementia. When she does, she will often say something inappropriate or even delusional. Once, believing she was on a train journey, probably across Italy, my mother asked me, 'Are you getting off at the next stop or staying on with me?' In this sort of surreal interchange, I always choose the most reassuring response to keep her happy; honesty is no longer the priority.

The phrase, 'like a baton or a wand' emphasises the sense of drama created by revealing the bag of chocolates. Although offering a chocolate is a simple act, it can transform the atmosphere, just as when an orchestra begins to play or a story character casts a magic spell. Here the feelings of frustration and powerlessness suddenly evaporate, if only for a few moments.

The poem begins objectively but the mood changes to reflect the close connection which is re-established. Sharing the experience of eating chocolate can be seen as a sort of communion. Love, as illustrated by the exchange of smiles, is at its centre. The final line, 'We have found a connection', has a triumphant tone.

Items Of Value

'Do you have any items of value?'
The nurse enquired.

The child's infectious giggle
The patient's warm smile
The farewell hug
The refreshing cup of water
The time spent listening
The morsel of bread
The signs of hope
Words of forgiveness
And the peace of God.

Items Of Value

Before going into a care home, my mother was admitted to hospital. At one point a nurse asked her, 'Do you have any items of value?' Being profoundly deaf, my mother had no idea that she had even been spoken to, so I replied on her behalf.

Sometimes it is humour which gets you through the most difficult times. As we waited for test results and to see if my mother's condition would stabilise, I began thinking about the expression 'items of value' and interpreting it in a different way. It is not the gold wedding ring or the precious silver locket which are of ultimate value when you are close to death. Such items can even become impediments. Rather, it is the less tangible things such as smiles, hugs and prayers which make us feel contented, encouraged and truly loved.

"Do not store up for yourselves treasures on earth, where moths and vermin destroy, and where thieves break in and steal. But store up for yourselves treasures in heaven, where moths and vermin do not destroy, and where thieves do not break in and steal. For where your treasure is, there your heart will be also."

(Matthew 6: 19-21)

Printed in August 2023
by Rotomail Italia S.p.A., Vignate (MI) - Italy